AF513294

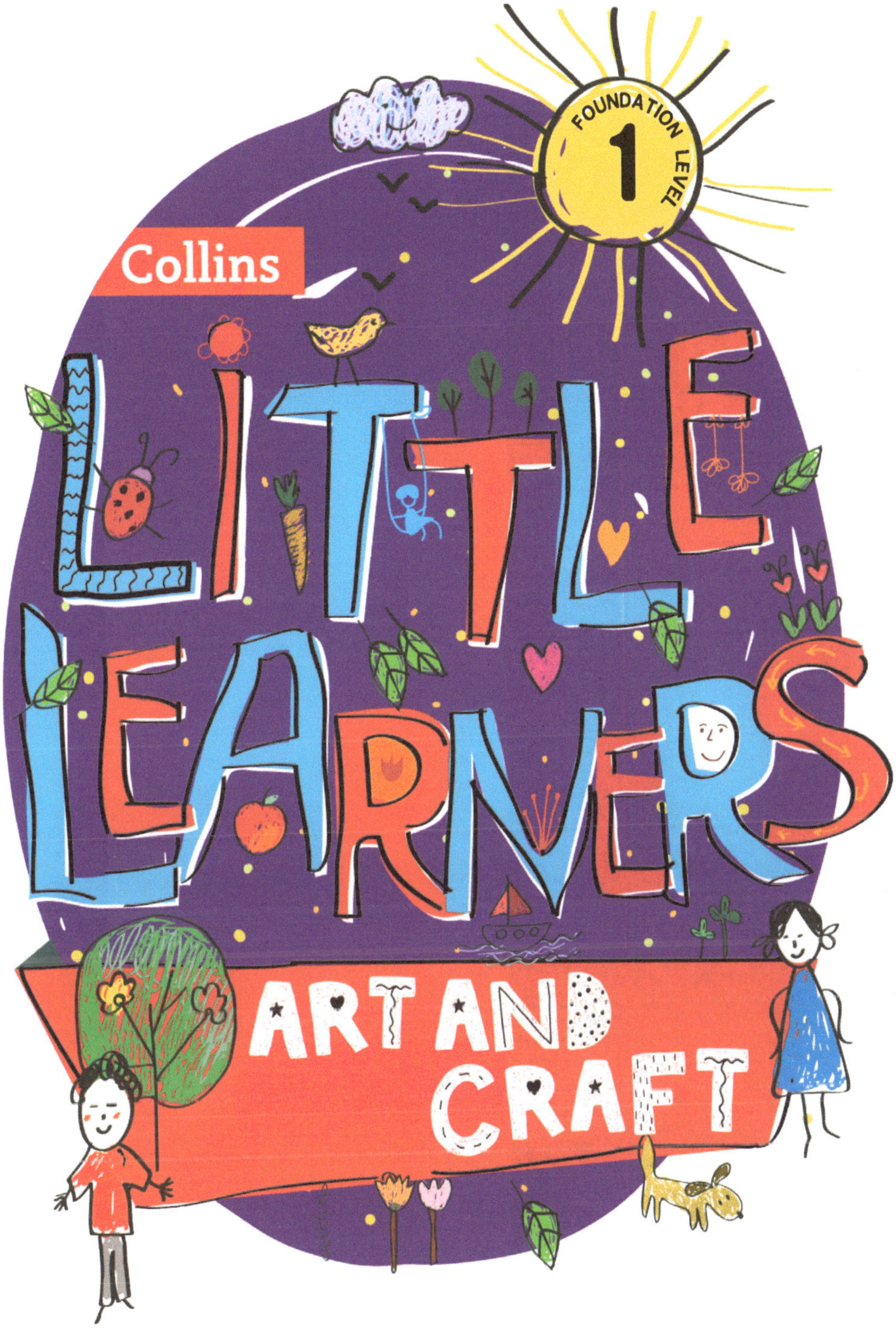


SERIES EDITOR: RANI T.

Published by Collins Learning
A division of HarperCollins*Publishers*
India Private Limited

HarperCollins Publishers
Building No. 10, Tower A, 4th Floor, DLF Cyber City, Gurugram, Haryana 122002, India

1 London Bridge Street, London, SE1 9GF, United Kingdom

2 Bloor Street East, Toronto, Ontario M4W 1A8, Canada

Lvl 13, 201 Elizabeth Street (PO Box A565, NSW, 1235), Sydney NSW 2000, Australia

195 Broadway, New York, NY 10007, USA

Browse the complete Collins catalogue at www.collins.in
For any queries/feedback, please write to us at **SCHOOLSUPPORT@harpercollins.co.in** or call us on **0120-4044800**.

First published in 2020
© HarperCollinsPublishers India Private Limited 2020
Re-print Edition-2025

ISBN: 978-935357-042-2

Collins ® is a registered trademark of HarperCollins*Publishers* Limited

All rights reserved. No part of this book may be reproduced, stored in retrieval system, or transmitted in any form or by any means, electronic, mechanical, photocopying, recording or otherwise, without the prior permission in writing of the Publisher. This book is sold subject to the conditions that it shall not, by way of trade or otherwise, be lent, re-sold, hired out or otherwise circulated without the publisher's prior consent in any form of binding or cover other than that in which it is published and without a similar condition including this condition being imposed on the subsequent purchaser.

Layout and Artwork by
Typeface Printographics Pvt. Ltd.

Printed and bound at Repro India Ltd.

## Acknowledgements

**Cover:** HarperCollins*Publishers*India
**Title Page:** HarperCollins*Publishers*India
**Prelim Pages:** radenmas, denkcreative, nonohana, graphic-bee
**Content created by:** Vasantha Priya, Jayanthi, Leela and Rachana

# Preface

**Collins Little Learners**, comprising 20 books in all, provides graded, age-appropriate learning opportunities targeting holistic skill development for children in the age group of 3 years to 6 years. Spread across three levels, the series spans **English**, **Maths**, **General Awareness**, **Art and Craft** and **Hindi**. The series comes bundled with a **workbook** for English and a book of **rhymes and stories** for each level. The books use a combination of hands-on activities, frequent recapitulation and child-friendly artwork to facilitate learning.

The early years are the most significant years for growth, development and learning. During this period, children need adequate opportunities for stimulating experiences as these favourably affect various learning abilities. Learning experiences, when chosen and planned properly, fuel the innate curiosity of children, and stimulate their thought processes.

## Learning and Development During the Early Years

The goal of learning during the early years is to enhance the all-round development of personality and to inculcate healthy attitudes, life skills and good values. Creative play, well thought-out games and developmentally appropriate activities help children develop the necessary skills to achieve these goals. The skills that children need to acquire can broadly be categorized as:

**Motor:** Motor skills pertain not only to gross motor activities like walking and jumping but also include fine motor activities like the ability to hold a pencil and write. The development of motor skills is facilitated through several graded activities.

**Personal, Social and Emotional:** Personal, social and emotional development, necessary for the overall personality development of children, is achieved using a combination of hands-on activities, role plays, and thought-provoking stories and rhymes.

**Linguistic:** The ability to listen, speak, read and write is critical to success in formal learning environments.

**Mathematical:** The development of mathematical ideas and concepts is important at this stage since children will continue to build on this learning for most of their years of schooling.

**Knowledge and Understanding of the World:** This is achieved through activities that enable children to explore their surroundings at home and in the school, and interact with the people that they see around them.

**Health and Safety:** The idea of health and safety is introduced through activities, stories and retelling of real-life experiences to encourage children to focus on health and well-being.

**Creative:** Creative skills are developed through a host of activities involving art, craft, painting, roleplays, etc.

**Logical and Rational Thinking:** Activities that involve simple puzzles, pattern-completion and visual discrimination help children develop logical and rational thinking skills.

## The Collins Little Learners Teacher Support Materials

The series includes extensive teacher support in the form of:

**Teacher's Resource Books:** Comprises stories, activity banks, classroom management and assessment guidelines

**Multimedia eBook:** Consists of animations, audio, video, slide shows, and interactive exercises

**Print-ready Worksheets:** Additional worksheets for practice and reinforcement, present in the digital support

**Digital Flashcards:** Flashcards with embedded sounds and animations for letter formation and letter-sound association

**Animations and Songs:** Animated stories and rhymes set to tune

**Interactive Games:** Interactivities to reinforce concepts in a fun and engaging manner

**A note on the activity banks (included in the Teacher's Manuals)**

The activity banks comprise hands-on activities that will help children develop the requisite skills to attain age-appropriate learning goals. In keeping with Howard Gardener's theory of multiple intelligences, the activity banks include options and variations that enable teachers to provide a planned cycle of experiences and opportunities, which foster each type of intelligence, to every child in their classrooms. The activity banks equip teachers to use the strengths of children as a means of complementing their less developed areas by valuing and nurturing the inherent abilities of the children.

# Contents

# Walkthrough

A variety of tracing and colouring activities to further fine motor development in an enjoyable manner

Free-hand drawing and colouring pages to support creative development

Rolling, flattening and shaping modelling clay and cotton to support motor development

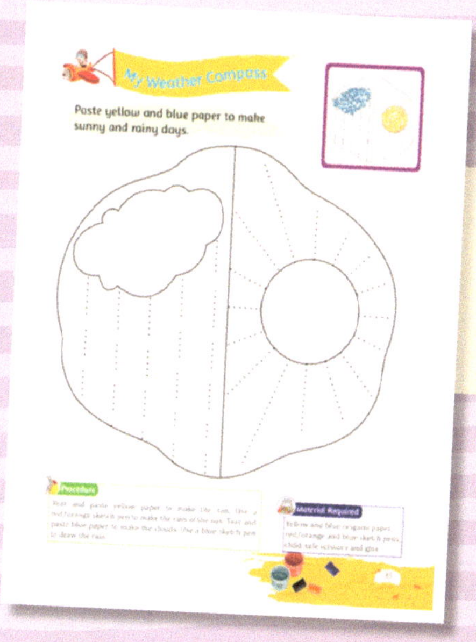


Tearing, pasting, cutting to improve hand-eye coordination and develop the ability to grip objects

Cross-curricular linkages in activities to help support overall learning and development

# Free-hand Scribbling

Colour the picture.

# Sticky Lollipops

Paste ice-cream sticks to make the lollipops.

**Material Required**

2 ice-cream sticks and glue

## Let's Colour!

Join the dots.
Colour the picture.

# Straw Ladders

Cut and paste straws to complete the ladders.

**Material Required**

3-4 straws, glue and child-safe scissors

## Let's Colour!

Join the dots. Colour the picture.

# Smiley Petals

**Paste correct number of stickers to make the petals for each flower.**

**Material Required**

Smiley stickers

**Procedure**

Paste the correct number of smiley stickers for each flower.

# I Can Colour!

Use crayons to colour.

# Clay Frolika

**Make balls of clay. Place them on the letter and the number.**

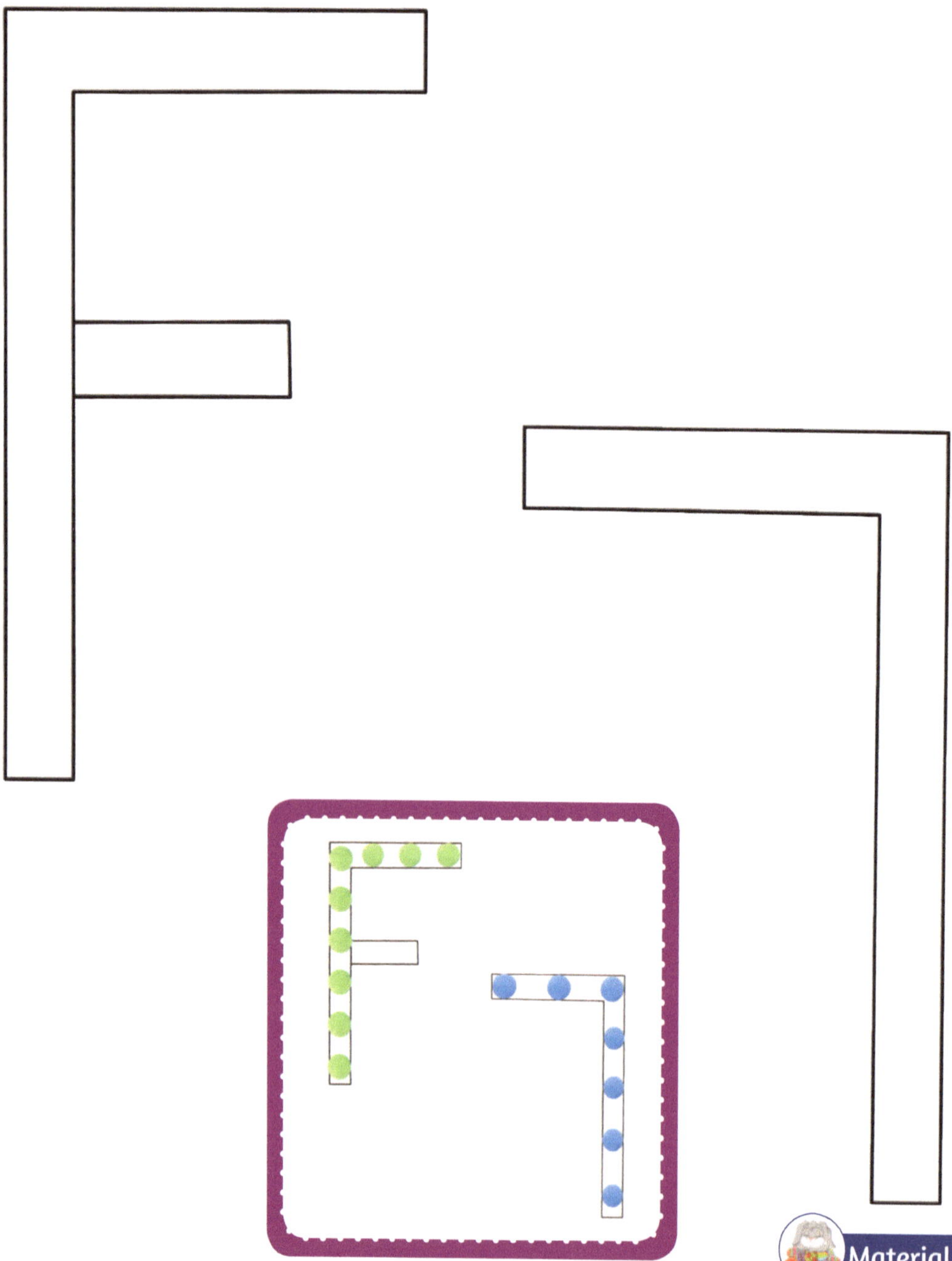

**Material Required**

Modelling clay and glue

**Procedure**

Use modelling clay to make small balls. Allow children to do this activity independently. They can then either place the balls on the letter or they can use glue to paste the balls on the page.

# Let's Draw!

Draw and colour anything you like.

# Hairy Monsters

Paste the correct number of strings to make the hair of these monsters.

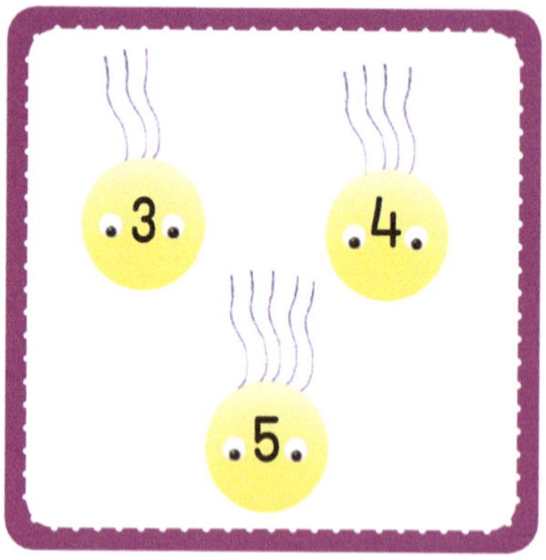

**Material Required**

Wool (of different colours), child-safe scissors and glue

# My Big Box of Insects

Fingerprint all the bugs in the box.

**Material Required**

Poster colours

**Procedure**

Use your fingers to print insects with different colours.

# Nature Walk

**Collect leaves and flowers from the garden.
Paste them in the vase.**

**Material Required**

Dry and fresh leaves / flowers and glue

**Procedure**

Take children for a walk in the garden. You can introduce them to varieties of flowers and they can collect dry and fresh leaves/flowers and paste it over the vase.

# Forky Flowers

Dip forks in paint and print to make forky flowers.

**Material Required**

1 fork, 2-3 poster colours and water

# Fluffy Rabbit

**Make cotton balls. Paste the balls on the rabbit.**

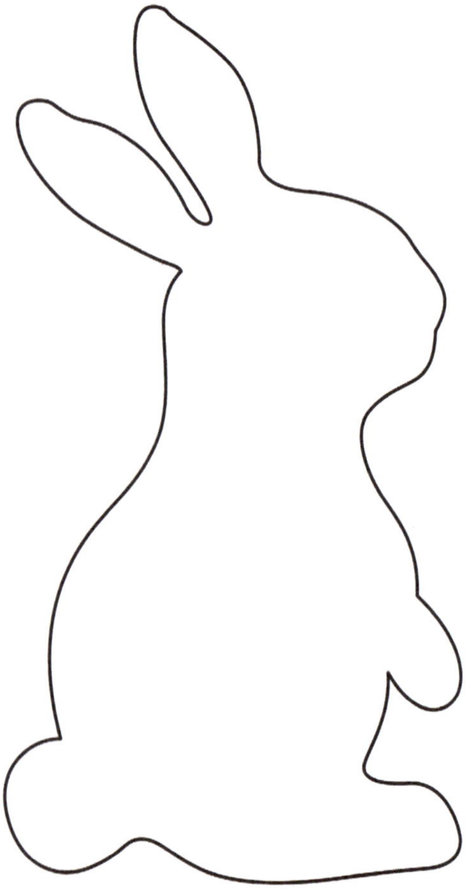

**Material Required**

Cotton, glue and googly eyes

**Procedure**

Roll the cotton to make balls. Paste these balls on the rabbit. At last, paste googly eyes on the rabbits.

# Let's Draw

Draw and colour anything you like.

# Shape Fun

Cut paper in different shapes. Paste it together to make an engine.

**Material Required**

Origami paper, glue and child-safe scissors

**Procedure**

Take differently coloured origami paper for different shapes. Cut the origami paper in the shapes of circle, square, rectangle and triangle. Guide children to paste the correct shape at the right place.

# Fun in the Rain

Make rain with blue wool.

**Material Required**

Blue wool, child-safe scissors and glue

# Clown's Hat

Paste coloured cotton balls on the clown's hat.

**Material Required**

Coloured cotton balls and glue

## Let's Colour!

Colour as you like.

# Lion in the Den

Make the den of the lion using modelling clay.

**Material Required**

Modelling clay and glue

# Pop Stick Chicks

**Paste ice-cream sticks to make chicks.**

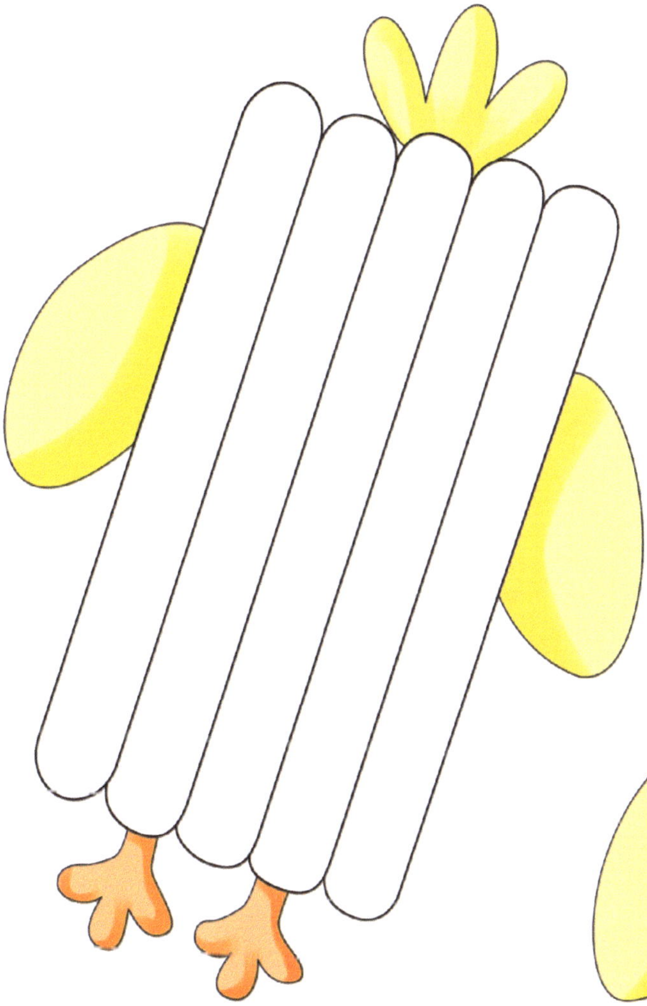

### Procedure

Paint ice-cream sticks using a paintbrush and yellow paint. Paste these sticks to make chicks. Paste googly eyes and triangular orange paper to complete the chicks.

### Material Required

Ice-cream sticks, yellow poster colour, 1 paintbrush, 4 googly eyes, triangular orange paper and glue

# Let's Colour!

**Colour as you like.**

# Woolly Sheep

Cut and paste lengths of wool to make the sheep.

**Material Required**

White wool, child-safe scissors and glue

# Wet Chalk Drawing

Use wet chalks to colour the pictures.

# Underwater World

**Paint your hand. Print it to make water animals.**

## Procedure

Ask children to dip their hands in yellow paint and print the shape of a fish and octopus (red paint) as shown in the figure. Use black sketch pen to make smiles for both the fish and the octopus.

## Material Required

Yellow and red poster colours, 3 googly eyes and black sketch pen

# My Weather Compass

**Paste yellow and blue paper to make sunny and rainy days.**

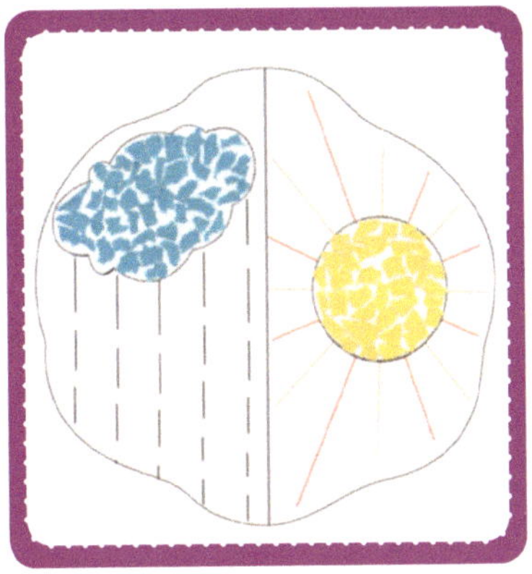

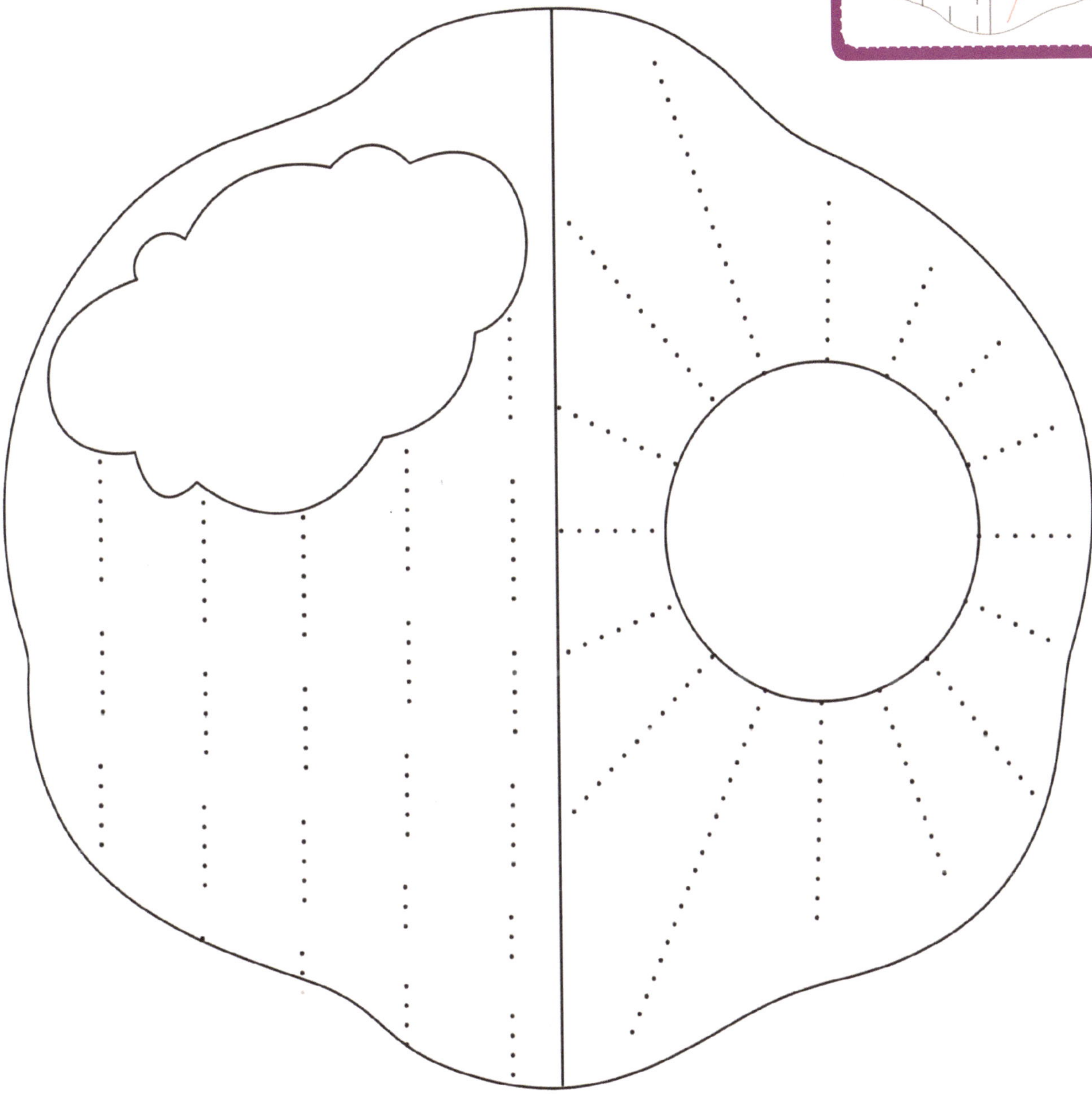

**Procedure**

Tear and paste yellow paper to make the sun. Use a red/orange sketch pen to make the rays of the sun. Tear and paste blue paper to make the clouds. Use a blue sketch pen to draw the rain.

**Material Required**

Yellow and blue origami paper, red/orange and blue sketch pens, child-safe scissors and glue

# The Night Sky

Paste stickers of stars.

**Material Required**

Stickers of stars

## Let's Draw!

Draw and colour anything you like.

# Beady Blinds

**Use straws and wool to make blinds. Decorate with beads.**

**Material Required**

5-10 straws, toothpick, wool, differently coloured beads, coloured paper, child-safe scissors and glue

**Procedure**

Cut straws into 3 in. long pieces. Thread the straws with wool. Alternate beads and straw pieces to make the blinds. Stick them on a straw. Paste on paper.

# Hi-Five Tree

Dip your hand in paint. Print your hand to make the tree.

**Material Required**

Light green and dark green poster colours

# Shelly Tortoise

**Paste pistachio shells to make the tortoise.**

### Material Required

Small paper plate, pistachio shells and glue

### Procedure

Paste an inverted, small paper plate on the tortoise. Paste pistachio shells on the paper plate to make the tortoise shell.

# Let's Colour!

Colour as you like.

# Making Snails Using Clay

**Material Required**

Modelling clay and glue

**Procedure**

Roll modelling clay into cylinders and paste to make the snail's shell.

# Dip And Print

**Fingerprint with different colours to make flowers and bees.**

**Material Required**

Poster colours

**Procedure**

Children can use poster colours of their choice to print flowers and bees.

# A Walk Along The Shore

Paste sand and shells to complete sandy beach.

**Material Required**

Dry sand, shells and glue

**Procedure**

Paste dry sand and shells to make the shore scene.

Colour as you like.

# Starry Ice Cream

**Paste ice-cream sticks and decorate with stickers to make the ice creams.**

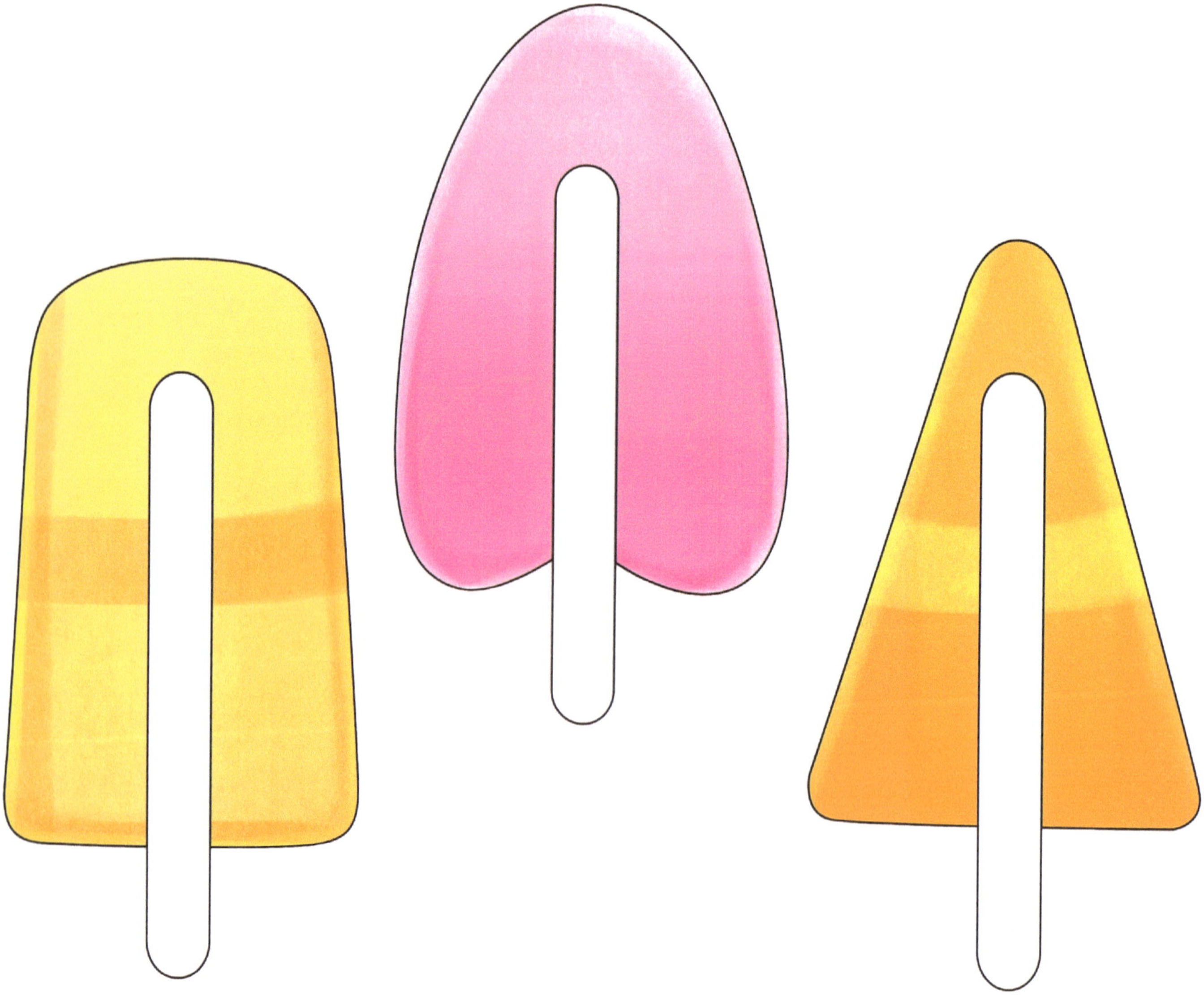

**Material Required**

Ice-cream sticks, decorative material like mirrors and stickers of stars, hearts and glue

**Procedure**

Paste an ice-cream stick for each ice cream. Decorate the ice creams with decorative material.

# Let's Colour!

Draw and colour anything you like.

# Best of Waste

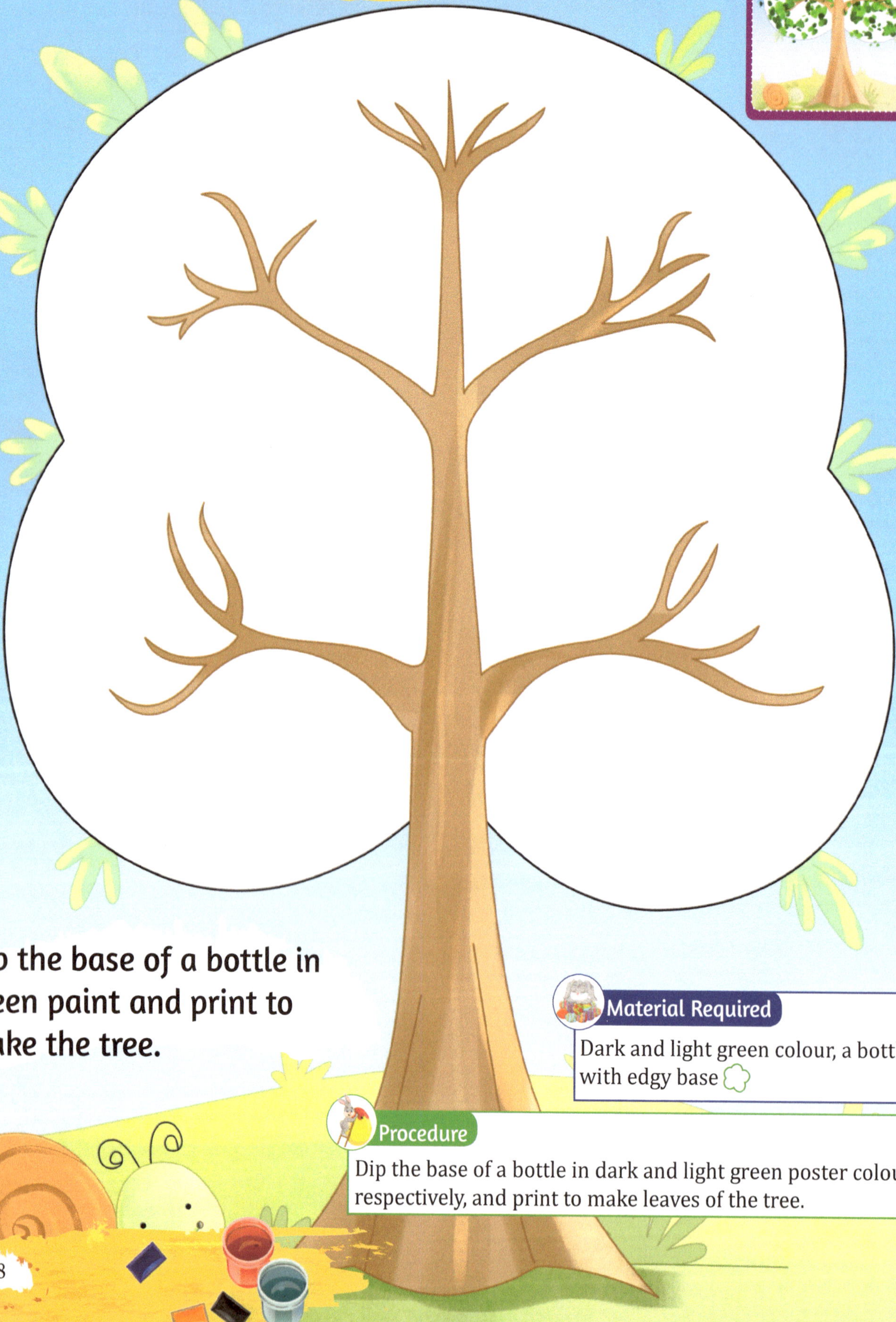

**Dip the base of a bottle in green paint and print to make the tree.**

**Material Required**

Dark and light green colour, a bottle with edgy base

**Procedure**

Dip the base of a bottle in dark and light green poster colours, respectively, and print to make leaves of the tree.